God's Attributes: Rest for of the character and attri knowledge of the God v

will guide you towards cultivating these character traits in your own life and to walk in faith before the God in whose likeness you are being transformed.

— **Daniel L. Akin,** President, Southeastern Baptist Seminary

Scripture tells us that "the name of the Lord is a strong tower; the righteous runs into it and is safe" (Prov. 18:10). Brad Hambrick captures this dual emphasis brilliantly by telling us to both rest in and emulate the marvelous attributes of God. This is a fine study that can be used to transform both heart and mind.

— **Gary Thomas,** Author, *The Glorious Pursuit: Embracing the Virtues of Christ*

A.W. Tozer famously said that what we think about God is the most important thing about us. Brad Hambrick has provided the church with a deeply theological, yet practically helpful tool for exploring the attributes of God, helping us see him more clearly and living in proper response. The "cycle of rest to emulation" model he proposes is pure gold. This is a life-changing study.

—**J. D. Greear,** The Summit Church, Durham, North Carolina

God's Attributes

The GOSPEL for REAL LIFE series

Brad Hambrick, Series Editor

God's Attributes

REST FOR LIFE'S STRUGGLES

BRAD HAMBRICK

PUBLISHING
P.O. BOX 817 • PHILLIPSBURG • NEW JERSEY 08865-0817

Printed in the United States of America

ISBN: 978-1-59638-415-6

HOW DO WE "DO THEOLOGY"? Do not read this as an academic question for people who have been to seminary—how *should* we do theology? Read it as an observational question about everyday people—how *do* we form our opinions and attitudes about God?

One portrayal of how we do theology is provided by breathing: inhale, process, and exhale. We inhale information, experiences, relationships, hopes, dreams, opportunities, tragedies, successes, failures, and an incredible number of mundane moments. These pieces are then processed by personal evaluations as good, bad, pleasant, unpleasant, painful, pleasurable, significant, noticed, or unnoticed. Finally, we exhale beliefs, correlations of cause and effect, life principles, optimistic or pessimistic expectations, and ideas about God (i.e., whoever or whatever we believe to be "in charge" of it all).

Consider a few examples. A kid wears stinky socks to his Little League baseball game because his mom was too busy to get the laundry done, and he hits a home run (events inhaled). Junior deems this experience to be good, pleasurable, and potentially leading to a life of fame and fortune (evaluations processed). At every game afterward, Junior wants to wear unwashed, stinky socks, lest "the baseball gods" curse him with being an ordinary little kid again (theology exhaled). Unfortunately, self-fulfilling prophecy—also known as con-fidence—has enough influence to frequently confirm Junior's theology.

As Junior grows up and gets a job, he leaves superstition behind and exchanges it for purpose. Realizing that not every-thing he wants to do can get done, he makes a list of everything that is being asked of him (events inhaled). Simple math tells him that all of this will not fit in a 168-hour week, so he deems these expectations unreasonable, bad, and stressful (evaluations processed). Crunching the numbers and the impact of giving attention to work, family, rest, and self, Junior creates a system that will please an abstract concept called "success" (exhale theology). For some period of time, Junior's obedience to, and deepening understanding of, the doctrine of success results in a blessed life.

Later Junior's life takes several turns for the worse that are no fault of his own: an illness, an economic downturn, a parent's death, his house robbed, an unfaithful spouse, or betrayal by a friend (events inhaled). With increasing fervor, Junior searches for some way to explain why these things happened, but can find no satisfying explanation (evaluations processed). Ultimately, he abandons the cause-and-effect beliefs of stinky socks and successful priorities, surrendering to the "reality" that life is random and meaningless (exhale theology). From that point onward, Junior's life begins to unravel as words like *good*, *worthwhile*, and *hope* lose their meaning.

As we can see, theology often goes by many names: superstition, purpose statements, priorities, meaning, hope, and explanations. And we have not even mentioned the Bible yet. The point so far is that we don't have to be intimidated by the word *theology*, because we all do it every day. Every day we assign meaning to life on the basis of some perception of ultimate reality. The goal from this point forward is to begin "breathing theology well."

As you prepare to get started, use the chart below to see better how you have been doing theology. A summary of Junior's examples is included in the chart to help you get the hang of it. Start with some of the formative events of your life. These major memories usually have the largest and most identifiable impact on our core beliefs (theology).

Inhale (Events)	Process (Evaluations)	Exhale (Theology)
Stinky socks and home run	Good and profitable	Cause and effect (lucky)
Too busy	Stressful and bad	Priorities earn success
Life tragedy	No answers	Life is meaningless

FROM LIFE TO GOD

So far, our discussion has hinted at direct beliefs about the person and character of God, focusing on how to live effectively and make sense of life. This is because most of us do not think we are defining God as we live. But we do.

In this study, which will become much more devotional, we will begin to look at sixteen attributes of God and see how our functional beliefs about life impact how we live. If you did not take time to reflect on the beliefs you gleaned from formative life events (chart above), it is worth the time to go back and do it. Until you clarify how you have thought, your ability to maintain the peace and joy of new beliefs will be significantly limited. It's as hard to fend off and alter the implications of beliefs you do not know you have as it is to punch a ghost.

As you reflect on these formative life events, the hard or negative ones will fit into one of two categories: sin or suffering. Sin encompasses those actions, beliefs, and emotions that are contrary to God's Word or character. Suffering includes the tragic and deteriorative effects of living in a fallen world, as well as the consequences of other's sin against you.

The guiding principle of this entire study is simply:

> Our battle *from* and *against* sin and suffering is first and foremost a battle *toward* and *for* God.

With this said, our concept of God, resulting from the theological breathing discussed above, greatly influences how we read the Bible. If we believe that God is a cosmic cop, we read the Bible fearfully wanting to know the things for which God will "pull us over" and for which he will "let us go"— the equivalent of the "how far over the speed limit can you drive and get away with it" debate. If we believe that God is a heavenly grandfather, then we read the Bible to find out what good ideas he has and how to stay on his good side to get the extra treats of his approval.

One of these images we do not trust. The other one we do not really need. According to research into what makes counseling effective, these are two of the most important variables: Does the individual believe that he or she needs help? Does the individual trust that the counselor can and will help him or her?

With this said, if we are going to read our Bibles effectively, we must know God accurately. Each time we breathe Scripture, just as when we breathe life, we must ask, "Is our interpretation accurate?" Chances are, we bring the same interpretive distortions to God and Scripture that we bring to life. We are continually going through the process described in Hebrews 5:14, "But solid food is for the mature, for those who have their powers of discernment trained by constant practice to distinguish good from evil." Good is simply a right view of God impacting life choices. Bad is the result of acting on a wrong view of God.

This is what it means to have our discernment trained to distinguish good from evil—that all of our actions, emotions, struggles, and failures should deepen our understanding of, trust in, reliance upon, and imitation of God's character. This study is designed to assist you in identifying the connections between your current life struggles and sins and the attributes of God you need to learn, clarify, trust, enjoy, or emulate more.

The premise of the exercise is:

> If, in our struggle to conquer sin and alleviate suffering, we fail to learn and treasure God more, we have missed the most important thing God is doing in the midst of these experiences.

Often people ask, "What is God trying to tell me in the midst of this?" Our particular answers to this question are usually rather speculative (depending on the accuracy of our general understanding of God's character and life). But we can know one thing that God is doing in every circumstance: revealing more of himself. Over ninety times in Scripture, God says of his actions something like "that they may know that I am the Lord."

When we miss this key interpretive principle of life and Scripture, we are bound to start or perpetuate some error. We may become rule-following, comfort-seeking Pharisees. We may become fearful children of an abusive, all-powerful parent. We may become haphazard pleasure seekers looking for good ideas in a random universe.

We need to be continually alert to these questions: Who is God? What is God like? How is God relevant and active in this moment? When we are alert to them, we can, by God's grace and self-revelation, become heart-focused, God-treasuring disciples of Christ.

ABOUT THIS STUDY

This study is designed to last at least four weeks. At first, it would be good to continue reading this booklet from start to finish, just as you would read an article, to get the big picture for the daily studies. On this first reading, you will not look up the Scripture references or try to answer the reflective questions.

Once you begin the devotional study, you will study one group of God's attributes per week. As you study an attribute, you will find a brief definition of it, several passages of Scripture that refer to it, and two sets of questions for self-assessment:

1. How well do I *rest* in this attribute of God? Do I take the appropriate degree of comfort and joy in this aspect of God's character?
2. How well do I *emulate* this attribute of God? As an image-bearer and ambassador of Christ, do I represent this attribute of God accurately to the world around me?

The order of these two sets of questions is intentional. First we demonstrate our belief that God is good by trusting him (the questions about rest). Then we exhibit this trust through the worship of imitation (questions about emulation). The four pieces of each day's study should create a cycle of purification for our beliefs about God and life:

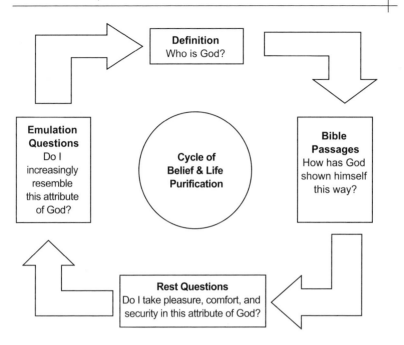

If you go through the study in a month (don't rush), then the first four days of the week you will study one attribute and evaluate yourself in light of it. On the fifth and sixth days, you will reflect upon how your understanding and application of God affect your current struggles—both suffering and sin. There are eight sets of questions at the end of each week to help you determine if your understanding of this collection of God's attributes makes your struggles better or worse, easier or harder, and in what ways. Wrestling with these questions will help your fleeing from sin and suffering to be a pursuit of God. On the seventh day, feel free to rest from this study.

Too often we read the Bible without asking the basic question, Who is God? We are looking for answers to other personal questions or are enamored by the drama and/or beauty of the text. There is great benefit to dedicating a month to focusing on God's person in the Bible and allowing all application and reflection to point us to him.

BEFORE YOU BEGIN

In the earlier written reflection, you were looking back. Now we want to come into the present. As you prepare for the study, make two lists of challenges you are currently facing: (1) your sufferings (hardships not the result of personal sin) and (2) your sins.

Current Struggles with Sin	Current Sources of Suffering

Take your time making these lists. They will serve as a point of reference for the rest of the study. Rightly understood and evaluated, our struggles in life will most often point us to and clarify the attributes of God we need to learn, rest in, treasure, and emulate more.

As you progress through the study, you may add to either list as you come to learn more about who God is and what he is like (thereby learning who we are to be as Christians and what we are to be like). This should become our standard habit of life—to look at God in order to learn how to rightly see ourselves and our world.

From this point forward, you may want to get a journal or notebook to record your reflections. An important part of this study will be to take time to review your notes. At the end of each week, you will be directed to compare your reflections in that section with your reflections in the other sections. It would also be useful to record your prayers, to see how your relationship with God develops as you progress through the study.

THE TWO INNER CIRCLES

Holiness

The inner hub of the circle on the following page represents the holiness of God. God's holiness consists of all of his attributes operating in perfect unity. Too often we think of God's holiness simply as his moral perfection. He is indeed morally perfect. However, we also need to emphasize the balance and symmetry of his perfections. Unless we do, our attempts to emulate God's character may result in unsustainable spurts of a particular virtue, rather than proportionate growth, where each facet of holiness supports the others.

While we will group the aspects of God's character under four headings (power, love, wisdom, and essence), his holiness means that there is no tension, friction, or contradiction between any of God's attributes. Holiness is all of God's perfections existing in perfect, joyous harmony, with each attribute completing and complementing the others.

Passages on God's holiness: Psalm 99; Isaiah 6; Matthew 5:43–48; 1 Peter 1:13–25.

Reflection. The implication is that if we find ourselves drawn to or emphasizing one attribute or group of attributes more than the others, we have distorted our understanding of God in a way that will likely manifest itself in the outer ring (problematic emotions or sinful behaviors). We do not get to choose the type of God we serve. God is one. We love and serve him as he is. We adjust to God; he does not change to our liking. *As you do this study, continually ask yourself this question: "Do I have a balanced view of God (i.e., a well-rounded circle) or is my view of God imbalanced (i.e., an oval or a blob)?"*

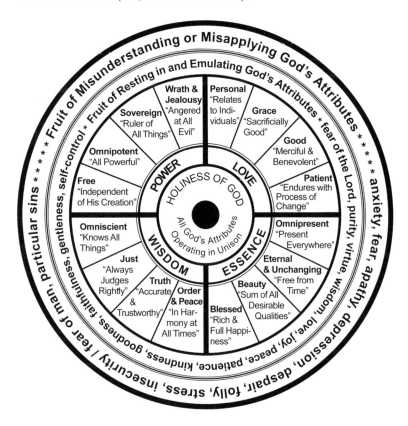

Four Quadrants

Theologians have many different methods of categorizing the attributes of God. The purpose of our grouping them into four quadrants in the above diagram is more practical than academic. There is more of an emphasis on what theologians call God's "positive attributes," "moral attributes," or "attributes of goodness" than on his "essence" or "greatness." This is because Christians, and many non-Christians, wrestle with what God does more than with who God is (James 1:19). Hopefully, as a part of this exercise, much of the artificial distinction between who God is and what God does will be eliminated.

WEEK ONE—ATTRIBUTES OF LOVE

Day One: God Is Personal

God has the ability to relate interpersonally, and he does so. God is neither aloof nor disinterested in his creation. God is aware of, and concerned about, the details of our lives. He is able to sympathize with the struggles we face in a fallen world. It is his nature to be active and involved.

Passages describing God as personal: Matthew 10:28–31; Psalm 56:8–11; Romans 8:26–27; Hebrews 4:14–16.

Diagnose resting in God as personal. Do you struggle to believe that God cares for you personally? Do you believe God only loves you generically (because he loves everybody)? Do you believe God is only concerned about the "big events" of your life, making the day-to-day choices drab or meaningless? Do you look for God in the small pleasantries of your day and express gratitude that he created a world with things that match your preferences and taste? *What would life and faith be like if God were not personal?*

Diagnose emulating God as personal. Do you avoid being vulnerable with others? When do you resist making yourself known because of a fear of rejection or of giving others power over you? How does this reveal a desire to be approved by people (the fear of man) that is greater than a desire to be approved by God (the fear of the Lord)? Are you skilled at using self-disclosure to make others feel comfortable and more willing to be vulnerable with you? *How does being personal open up conversation toward God and the gospel?*

Day Two: God Is Grace

God seeks our greatest good, even at his own infinite cost. Every good thing that God does for us is rooted in his delight in loving, not in the merit of our efforts to get his attention or obtain blessings from him. God gives undeserved pardon for our sins and unearned supply for every one of our true needs. He is faithful to sustain us in the midst of every hardship, whether they be hardships of suffering or of sin. With regard to salvation and spiritual growth, God overcomes our inadequacies by the sufficiency of his grace and does not resent doing so.

Passages describing God as grace: 1 John 4:7–12; Ephesians 2:1–10; Titus 2:11–14.

Diagnose resting in God as grace. Are there certain sins (that you have committed) that you believe God is less inclined to forgive? Is there a human relationship in which you can find something that compares to God's grace? Do you struggle with guilt or shame because you treat grace as something you must pay back? If so, what criteria do you try to meet to pay God back or to earn his acceptance? What is it that you think God won't forgive? Are there certain things about other people that make them "more lovable" in God's eyes? *What would life and faith be like if God were not grace?*

Diagnose emulating God as grace. Are you harsh or ambivalent toward those who fail or struggle? Do you harbor resentment and bitterness? Are there types of sins you are unwilling to forgive? What pet peeves do you expect others to adhere to if they are going to be close to you? Do you view emulating his grace as weakness or permissiveness and therefore struggle to emulate it? Are you a perfectionist? Do you expect the performance of others always to be improving? *How does emulating grace open up conversation toward God and the gospel?*

Day Three: God Is Good

God is the ultimate standard of what it means to be good. Everything that can be genuinely defined as good is, in some way, a reflection of God's character. More than success, comfort, pleasure, or unity, God's character is the standard of what is good. When we say something is good, we are saying it is like God in some way. God does not need words like *better* or *best* because his worth and standard are not in competition with anyone or anything.

Passages describing God as good: Luke 18:18–30; Psalm 107; Psalm 34:8–22.

Diagnose resting in God as good. Are you angry with God, believing he has not been good to you? Do you feel cheated by the things you cannot do as a Christian? Do you live as if God must prove his goodness to you before you will believe it? Do you spend time thinking about how you would have done things if you were God? When you receive compliments from others, do you hear the meaning "resembling God" in their synonyms for *good*? *What would life and faith be like if God were not good?*

Diagnose emulating God as good. Is your obedience to God more rooted in duty ("I have to") than delight ("I want to")? Does your obedience to God's commands give you the opportunity to discuss their goodness (e.g., their beauty, protection, order, wisdom, balance, and completeness)? Can you have these conversations about the goodness of God's commands with the genuineness, vividness, and passion with which you talk about your other major interests? Are you embarrassed when your actions coincide with God's good more than culture's cool? *How does being good open up conversation toward God and the gospel?*

Day Four: God Is Patient

God is slow to anger, graciously allowing time for repentance and change. While God will not be mocked with false repentance, he does not meet our every failure immediately with its due consequence (whether we are believers or unbelievers). God is not rushed into action by any sense of insecurity or threat. God acts only when it is right and good to do so. God displays his power through the restraint of his loving patience.

Passages describing God as patient: Romans 2:1–11; Jonah 4; Exodus 34:6–9.

Diagnose resting in God as patient. Do you wonder when God will give up on you? Do you fear that God will get tired of hearing your requests or is annoyed by your prayers? When do you feel pressure from God to "get" or "do" something that is really hard for you? Do you resent God's patience in dealing with someone who has hurt you or someone with whom you are competing? Do you misinterpret God's patience to mean that he ignores or condones your sin? *What would life and faith be like if God were not patient?*

Diagnose emulating God as patient. What sins or irritants illicit quick anger in you? Of what types of people or actions are you least patient? Is your lack of patience rooted in false belief (that certain sins are worse), a lack of self-control (ability to enact true beliefs), or pride (anger at having to wait)? Do people feel safe to make mistakes around you? What activities or events consume you and make it hard to wait? Do you feel offended if you have to wait? *How does being patient open up conversation toward God and the gospel?*

Days Five and Six: Reflecting on God's Love

Without reflection, study is either lost (forgotten) or neglected (never acted upon). This study is designed to facilitate long-standing change, deeply rooted in worship. The following questions are good for personal reinforcement, small-group discussion, or deeper evaluation with a pastor or counselor.

1. Which of the attributes in this quadrant do you rest in best? Which do you emulate best? Give examples and allow yourself to be encouraged by these evidences of God's presence in your life. Which of the attributes in this quadrant do you struggle most to rest in? Which do you emulate least? Give examples and make these areas of prayer. Treat these examples as prime ground for new fruit in your life.

2. Which of the attributes in this quadrant do you still struggle to understand or truly believe? What questions do you have about these attributes? Where do these questions come from? How long have you held these questions?

3. How do you see your understanding of, reliance upon, and emulation of these attributes contributing to the fruit of the Spirit and skillful wisdom in your life (see the next to last circle in the quadrant diagram)?

4. What connections do you see between your struggles/sins and a misunderstanding of, a lack of rest in, or poor

emulation of these attributes of God (see the outermost circle in the quadrant diagram)?

5. What relationships, experiences, or beliefs contribute to your struggles to rest in or emulate these attributes of God? How might this reveal "making God in the image of man"? Who does this reveal that you are emulating (out of admiration or fear) other than God?

6. How does your understanding of, rest in, and emulation of this quadrant of attributes compare to that of the other three quadrants? How balanced is your view of God (a circle, an oval, or a blob)?

7. What changes do you need to make to understand or rely upon these attributes of God more? What specific actions (i.e., repentance, study, changing life patterns, or learning new skills) will this require? Who is holding you accountable? Whose advice or counsel are you seeking?

8. How would you summarize the changes in your view of God as a result of this week's study? What hope, relief, joy, or fear of the Lord has emerged from those changes?

The Main Point

Take time to praise God for how effortlessly he manifests all these qualities. Our struggles to rest in and emulate God's character should serve to increase our level of awe and deep appreciation for the God we have the privilege of serving. As you study Scripture, sing hymns and songs, interact with people, and live in creation, look and listen for these attributes. Praise God when you find them.

WEEK TWO—ATTRIBUTES OF ESSENCE

Day One: God Is Omnipresent

God is present everywhere. Just as he is not limited by time, so is he not limited by space. God is equally present (with all of his attributes and abilities) in all places at all times. To experience

God's presence is simply a matter of awareness and appreciation, not petition or request. There is no delay in God's response to any situation because he has to regroup or gather himself.

Passages describing God as omnipresent: Psalm 139:7–12; Jeremiah 23:23–24; Acts 17:28; Colossians 1:17.

Diagnose resting in God as omnipresent. Do you feel alone or abandoned by God? Do you sin in certain places or on certain occasions because you think "no one will know"? Do you feel like you must be in certain places to really connect with God? How does resting in God's omnipresence allow for focus or security wherever you are? Do you fear certain places as being "God forsaken"? *What would life and faith be like if God were not omnipresent?*

Diagnose emulating God as omnipresent. Do you struggle to be "all there" with certain tasks or relationships? Do you feel like life depends on you to continue or to function properly? Do you find that you start and not finish tasks because you get distracted? What things most often pull you away from the moment you are in? Who or what do you have the hardest time being there for? *How does being fully present and focused open up conversation toward God and the gospel?*

Day Two: God Is Eternal and Unchanging

God is free from time and the effects of time. He is the same yesterday, today, and tomorrow. He does not experience aging or an increase in knowledge. He sees all points in history equally vividly and with the same degree of certainty. God is not affected by trends or changes in culture.

Passages describing God as eternal and unchanging: 2 Peter 3:8–13; Isaiah 46:9–10; Hebrews 13:8.

Diagnose resting in God as eternal and unchanging. Are you concerned that God will change the "rules of life" or that modern times have made him obsolete? Do you take comfort in the constancy of God's character and expectations? How is that different from all other relationships? How does his being unchanging make it worthwhile to learn to follow his ways? *What would life and faith be like if God were not eternal and unchanging?*

Diagnose emulating God as eternal and unchanging. How consistent are your expectations of others? How consistent are your views about important aspects of life? How quickly do you grow bored with relationships, purchases, or activities? Are you fickle? Are you content? Can you articulate the timeless values upon which you make decisions? Do you regard being stubborn in your sin or your selfishness the same as being unchanging like God? *How does being consistent open up conversation toward God and the gospel?*

Day Three: God Is Beauty

God is the glorious sum of all desirable attributes. Everything that should create awe, joy, inspiration, devotion, and excitement has its origin and culmination in God. Anything that creates these dispositions that is not pointing us to God is competing with him, and thereby distracting our worship (idolatry). All legitimate beauty in creation is the reflection or fingerprint of its Creator.

Passages describing God as beauty: Psalm 27:4; Psalm 73:25; Revelation 22:1–5.

Diagnose resting in God as beauty. Is God your treasure and joy? Do you feel pressure to live up to an external definition of beauty or one rooted in godliness (1 Peter 3:4)? Do you punish and degrade yourself or base your confidence upon changes in your outward appearance, abilities, or popularity? Does the bodily deterioration of age cause you fear? Do you think of your "beauty" as particular evidence of God's presence in your life? *What would life and faith be like if God were not beauty?*

Diagnose emulating God as beauty. Do you evaluate others primarily on the basis of their appearance, ability, or popularity? Do you take care of your body, mind, and emotions to present a healthy and complete portrait of beauty? How does beauty drive, entice, or discourage you? Do you give balanced compliments to others based upon all facets of beauty or just physical appearance? Is your appreciation of beauty an intentional hunt for, and celebration of, God's essence? *How does emulating beauty open up conversation toward God and the gospel?*

Day Four: God Is Blessed

God is infinitely and richly happy in all that reflects his character. Within himself as the Trinity, God is without need or want. His joy and pleasures are robust and full. His disposition toward all that reflects his character is deeply satisfied. Heaven is the place where we all join with God completely in reflecting and enjoying his character.

Passages describing God as blessed: 1 Timothy 6:15; Genesis 1:31; Isaiah 62:5.

Diagnose resting in God as blessed. Do you view God as richly happy or as reserved, somber, and stoic? Do you believe heaven is a place you will enjoy or one that is merely ornate and beautiful? Do you believe God has truly designed and offers the fullest life possible (because he could do no less)? Does your view of God's disposition influence whether you truly believe you can be fully happy in God? Do you view God as being "needy" in order to justify the neediness you feel in relationships? *What would life and faith be like if God were not blessed and richly happy?*

Diagnose emulating God as blessed. What do you require to be happy? About what do you say, "If only . . ."? What do your experiences of joy teach you about your heart, what you worship, and what you live for? How do you try to use other people or these experiences to foster a sense of happiness independent of God? Do you believe it is less than spiritual to express joy, happiness, or excitement? What joys do you feel guilty about? *How does being blessed and richly happy open up conversation toward God and the gospel?*

Days Five and Six: Reflecting on God's Essence

Without reflection, study is either lost (forgotten) or neglected (never acted upon). This study is designed to facilitate long-standing change, deeply rooted in worship. The following questions are good for personal reinforcement, small-group discussion, or deeper evaluation with a pastor or counselor.

1. Which of the attributes in this quadrant do you rest in best? Which do you emulate best? Give examples and allow yourself to be encouraged by these evidences of God's presence in your life. Which of the attributes in this quadrant do you struggle most to rest in? Which do you emulate least? Give examples and make these areas of prayer. Treat these examples as prime ground for new fruit in your life.

2. Which of the attributes in this quadrant do you still struggle to understand or truly believe? What questions do you have about these attributes? Where do these

questions come from? How long have you held these questions?

3. How do you see your understanding of, reliance upon, and emulation of these attributes contributing to the fruit of the Spirit and skillful wisdom in your life (see the next to last circle in the quadrant diagram)?

4. What connections do you see between your struggles/ sins and a misunderstanding of, a lack of rest in, or poor emulation of these attributes of God (see the outermost circle in the quadrant diagram)?

5. What relationships, experiences, or beliefs contribute to your struggles to rest in or emulate these attributes of God? How might this reveal "making God in the image of man"? Who does this reveal that you are emulating (out of admiration or fear) other than God?

6. How does your understanding of, rest in, and emulation of this quadrant of attributes compare to that of the other three quadrants? How balanced is your view of God (a circle, an oval, or a blob)?

7. What changes do you need to make to understand or rely upon these attributes of God more? What specific actions (i.e., repentance, study, changing life patterns, or learning new skills) will this require? Who is holding you accountable? Whose advice or counsel are you seeking?

8. How would you summarize the changes in your view of God as a result of this week's study? What hope, relief, joy, or fear of the Lord has emerged from those changes?

The Main Point

Take time to praise God for how effortlessly he manifests all these qualities. Our struggles to rest in and emulate God's character should serve to increase our level of awe and deep appreciation for the God we have the privilege of serving. As you study Scripture, sing hymns and songs, interact with people, and live in creation, look and listen for these attributes. Praise God when you find them.

WEEK THREE—ATTRIBUTES OF WISDOM

Day One: God Is Order and Peace

God operates without confusion or disorder. In the infinite number of functions that God is always carrying out, he is fully controlled and without fretting. God's actions are not random or based on whims of emotion. His perpetual disposition is one of rest, not anxiety or worry. In the same way that plants process carbon dioxide into oxygen and animals process oxygen into carbon dioxide, all of God's activities aid and give life to the others.

Passages describing God as order and peace: 1 Corinthians 14:33; Romans 15:33; Philippians 4:9.

Diagnose resting in God as order and peace. Are you fearful that God will place competing expectations on you? How do you respond to seeming contradictions? Do you view the Bible as a confusing list of rules? Can you identify and rejoice in the guiding themes of Scripture? Are you awed by the balance and interdependence of God's creation? Do you pay more attention to the disruptions of order and peace caused by the Fall or to the pervasive order and peace of God that withstands sin's influence? *What would life and faith be like if God were not order and peace?*

Diagnose emulating God as order and peace. Do you exhibit self-control and intentionality in making decisions? Does impulsiveness cause you regret? What impulses most frequently disrupt the order and peace of your life? Do the basic systems of your life provide order and peace (e.g., worship, budget, schedule, communication, diet, recreation, rest, study, service)? Are your relationships marked by peace or strife? *How does emulating order and peace open up conversation toward God and the gospel?*

Day Two: God Is Truth

God is the final standard of truth. Truth is the reality that God created. All that he does and says is consistent, accurate, and reliable. Wherever truth is, God is present. All things that are false are in contradiction to, or in competition with, God. Learning, regardless of subject matter, is a holy enterprise by which we seek to accurately understand the character and work of God. Indifference toward the truth is indifference toward God.

Passages describing God as truth: John 14:5–14; Jeremiah 10:10–13; Proverbs 30:5.

Diagnose resting in God as truth. Do you feel like you must prove or defend the Bible in order for it to be true? Do you get anxious when someone raises a question about God or the Bible that you do not know how to answer? Do you wonder if it is possible to know things for certain, or if there are moral absolutes? Do you regard other sources of knowledge as equal to God's Word? Do you wonder whether God will keep his promises in Scripture? Do you reserve the right to decide what parts of God's Word you will believe or obey? *What would life and faith be like if God were not truth?*

Diagnose emulating God as truth. Do you let your yes be yes and your no be no (Matt. 5:37)? Do you speak the same way (in content and tone) around different types of people? Are

you regularly evaluating your beliefs, priorities, and practices
biblically to avoid contradicting yourself? Are you skilled at
speaking clearly what you intend to say, taking into consider-
ation how the listener will receive it? Do you enjoy learning?
*How does emulating truth open up conversation toward God and
the gospel?*

Day Three: God Is Just

God displays moral equity and does not show favoritism.
He ensures that the penalty for every moral injustice is paid
in full, either at Calvary or in hell. God's moral standard and
enforcement are perfect. He is never mocked by the oversight of,
or casualness toward, evil of any kind. While we are trapped in
time, it may be hard for us to see God's justice, but it is depend-
able. He delights more in repentance as a means to restoration
(Calvary) than in punishment as a means to moral satisfaction
(hell).

Passages describing God as just: Psalm 19; Job 40; Acts 10:34–35.

Diagnose resting in God as just. Do you find yourself question-
ing God when you are sinned against? Do the great injustices
of history and current events cause you to doubt God? Does
bitterness leave you wanting to be judge in God's place? Does
your life have a tone of "that's not fair"? Are you willing to
"leave it to the wrath of God" (Rom. 12:19)? Do you allow the
governing authorities to fulfill their role as temporal agents of
God's justice and wrath (Rom. 13:4)? *What would life and faith
be like if God were not just?*

Diagnose emulating God as just. Are you fair, balanced, and
gracious in your evaluations of others? Do you exaggerate or
understate the standards you hold yourself to as compared to
others? Are you consistent in the administration of punish-

ment when you are in a position of authority? Do your times of judgment leave room for, and point toward, the cross? Do you view repentance as a cop-out for not following through on discipline? Are you prone to accept repentance without fruit because of your dislike for administering discipline or justice? *How does being just open up conversation toward God and the gospel?*

Day Four: God Is Omniscient

God knows all things actual and possible, completely and without strain of memory. God does not fail to act in a particular way because he did not consider the possibility and its contingencies. God does not forget. He never fails to act or sympathize because of a lack of knowledge. He does not overlook or neglect details. He does not emphasize some facts to the neglect of others.

Passages describing God as omniscient: Psalm 139:1–4; Hebrews 4:12–13; 1 John 3:16–20.

Diagnose resting in God as omniscient. Do you ever feel like no one understands you? Are you intimidated by being known completely? Do you find peace in the fact that the God who knows all makes himself and his ways known in a way that is sufficient for life and godliness (2 Peter 1:3–5)? Do your fears assume that something is coming for which God is not prepared or will not prepare you? When you hear of "new findings" in science or other fields, does that cause you to be nervous about your faith? *What would life and faith be like if God were not omniscient?*

Diagnose emulating God as omniscient. Are you consistent and diligent in your study of Scripture, people, and life? Do you take joy in learning? Do you approach times of study as moments to reflect more on God's character or creation? Can you teach (even those who struggle to learn) without growing impatient or self-righteous? Are you gullible or naïve? Do you focus on single subjects or facts to the neglect of other important material? *How does being wise and always learning open up conversation toward God and the gospel?*

Days Five and Six: Reflecting on God's Wisdom

Without reflection, study is either lost (forgotten) or neglected (never acted upon). This study is designed to facilitate long-standing change, deeply rooted in worship. The following questions are good for personal reinforcement, small-group discussion, or deeper evaluation with a pastor or counselor.

1. Which of the attributes in this quadrant do you rest in best? Which do you emulate best? Give examples and allow yourself to be encouraged by these evidences of God's presence in your life. Which of the attributes in this quadrant do you struggle most to rest in? Which do you emulate least? Give examples and make these areas of prayer. Treat these examples as prime ground for new fruit in your life.

2. Which of the attributes in this quadrant do you still struggle to understand or truly believe? What questions do you have about these attributes? Where do these questions come from? How long have you held these questions?

3. How do you see your understanding of, reliance upon, and emulation of these attributes contributing to the fruit of the Spirit and skillful wisdom in your life (see the next to last circle in the quadrant diagram)?

4. What connections do you see between your struggles/ sins and a misunderstanding of, a lack of rest in, or poor

emulation of these attributes of God (see the outermost circle in the quadrant diagram)?

5. What relationships, experiences, or beliefs contribute to your struggles to rest in or emulate these attributes of God? How might this reveal "making God in the image of man"? Who does this reveal that you are emulating (out of admiration or fear) other than God?

6. How does your understanding of, rest in, and emulation of this quadrant of attributes compare to that of the other three quadrants? How balanced is your view of God (a circle, an oval, or a blob)?

7. What changes do you need to make to understand or rely upon these attributes of God more? What specific actions (i.e., repentance, study, changing life patterns, or learning new skills) will this require? Who is holding you accountable? Whose advice or counsel are you seeking?

8. How would you summarize the changes in your view of God as a result of this week's study? What hope, relief, joy, or fear of the Lord has emerged from those changes?

The Main Point

Take time to praise God for how effortlessly he manifests all these qualities. Our struggles to rest in and emulate God's character should serve to increase our level of awe and deep appreciation for the God we have the privilege of serving. As you study Scripture, sing hymns and songs, interact with people, and live in creation, look and listen for these attributes. Praise God when you find them.

WEEK FOUR—ATTRIBUTES OF POWER

Day One: God Is Free

God is independent of his creation. We cannot make claims on God. Based upon the constancy of his character and actions, we have assurance of how he will act. But God is a debtor to no one and is under no obligation other than to be consistent with his character. God has no negative emotions that would compel him to act for the purpose of gaining relief.

Passages describing God as free: Psalm 115:3; Proverbs 21:1; Daniel 4:35.

Diagnose resting in God as free. Do you believe you must know why God did something? Can you be satisfied knowing that God's actions are consistent with his character, even if you do not understand his objective? Does God's freedom scare you? Is your obedience a means of trying to control God instead of worshipping him? Do you find peace in the fact that no one can pressure or blackmail God? *What would life and faith be like if God were not free?*

Diagnose emulating God as free. Do you desire a freedom that would allow you to act outside God's revealed will? Does God's character seem restrictive to your personal expression and preferences? Do you place yourself in bondage to habits, substances, creditors, or people's opinions? Are you motivated by the avoidance of guilt or by delighting in the things that are right and good? Do you embrace forgiveness as a means of dealing with regret or do you try to hide, forget, or drown out those memories? *How does being free open up conversation toward God and the gospel?*

Day Two: God Is Omnipotent

God is all-powerful. He is completely capable of completing every aspect of his holy will. There is no situation that will arise in which God will need to act, but be unable to do so. There is no evil so great that God cannot redeem it. He does not wear out or grow exhausted. He is always under control and is never intimidated. He is never in a position that requires him to negotiate or make a deal.

Passages describing God as omnipotent: Jeremiah 32:17; Ephesians 3:20; Luke 1:37.

Diagnose resting in God as omnipotent. Do you wonder if God is able to redeem your suffering or provide victory over your sin? What is it about your suffering or sin that seems beyond God's ability? What does this reveal about how you are thinking about your suffering or sin? Do you have a tendency to wrongly "trust God" with things that are your responsibility? What prayers are you hesitant to pray? *What would life and faith be like if God were not omnipotent?*

Diagnose emulating God as omnipotent. Do you tend to abuse or neglect your expressions of boldness and confidence? How well do you manifest having "a spirit . . . of power" (2 Tim. 1:7)? Do you assume failure? Are you easily intimidated? Do you make deals in order to establish or maintain a position of advantage? When are you tempted to believe you cannot "stand firm" against, or find "the way of escape" from, temptation because it is too strong (Eph. 6:13; 1 Cor. 10:13)? *How does rightly exercising power and being confident open up conversation toward God and the gospel?*

Day Three: God Is Sovereign

God is the supreme ruler of his creation. He is the author of history and has inspired the writing of Scripture. Before the foundation of the world, he declared that people from every nation would be his, and he is guiding history to that God-exalting end. God owns everything—first, by right of creation, and second, by purchasing it with the blood of his Son at Calvary.

Passages describing God as sovereign: Ephesians 1; Acts 4:24–31; 1 Timothy 6:13–16.

Diagnose resting in God as sovereign. Do you struggle with a sense that life is out of control, that there is no guiding purpose or direction to the events of history (or your personal life)? Are you superstitious? Does this reveal an agenda that competes with God's will or ambivalence toward his agenda? When do you lose hope? Does God's sovereignty make you unduly passive? *What would life and faith be like if God were not sovereign?*

Diagnose emulating God as sovereign. Do you live for the glory of God (1 Cor. 10:31–33)? Do you take joy in evaluating your gifts, abilities, and passions to determine how God has designed you to play a part in his plan for history? Do you feel cheated that life is for God's glory, not yours? Do you rule your corner of creation in a way that displays God's character to those under your authority? *How does joyfully submitting to God's sovereignty open up conversation toward God and the gospel?*

Day Four: God Is Wrath and Jealousy

God seeks to protect his honor and intensely hates anything that rivals or seeks to replace his supremacy. God does not take worship lightly. When we regard anything, other than God himself, as utmost in our affections, we will face the heat of God's displeasure. Nothing is more satisfying than God; therefore, when we seek pleasure outside of him, God is jealous for our good and his glory.

Passages describing God as wrath and jealousy: Exodus 34:13–17; Romans 1:18–27; Psalm 103.

Diagnose resting in God as wrath and jealousy. Do you see the evil around you without fear, knowing that evildoers will

either repent or be adequately punished? Does a keen awareness of God's jealousy and wrath keep you from sin? Do you
view your sin as moments of worshipping other gods (e.g.,
self, pleasure, or approval), taunting God's reign in your life?
Do you view God's wrath as a good attribute, protecting you
from folly? *What would life and faith be like if God were not
wrath and jealousy?*

Diagnose emulating God as wrath and jealousy. What things
most commonly make you angry or jealous? Are they violations
of the law of God or pet peeves (your law)? Do you express your
anger in a manner that is proportionate to the infraction? Do
you express anger in a manner that is in balance with the other
attributes of God? When you get angry, do people realize it
is God's honor you are protecting (Num. 20:1–13)? *How does
emulating wrath and jealousy open up conversation toward God
and the gospel?*

Days Five and Six: Reflecting on God's Power

Without reflection, study is either lost (forgotten) or neglected (never acted upon). This study is designed to facilitate
long-standing change, deeply rooted in worship. The following
questions are good for personal reinforcement, small-group discussion, or deeper evaluation with a pastor or counselor.

1. Which of the attributes in this quadrant do you rest in
   best? Which do you emulate best? Give examples and
   allow yourself to be encouraged by these evidences of
   God's presence in your life. Which of the attributes in
   this quadrant do you struggle most to rest in? Which do
   you emulate least? Give examples and make these areas
   of prayer. Treat these examples as prime ground for new
   fruit in your life.

2. Which of the attributes in this quadrant do you still struggle to understand or truly believe? What questions do you have about these attributes? Where do these questions come from? How long have you held these questions?

3. How do you see your understanding of, reliance upon, and emulation of these attributes contributing to the fruit of the Spirit and skillful wisdom in your life (see the next to last circle in the quadrant diagram)?

4. What connections do you see between your struggles/ sins and a misunderstanding of, a lack of rest in, or poor emulation of these attributes of God (see the outermost circle in the quadrant diagram)?

5. What relationships, experiences, or beliefs contribute to your struggles to rest in or emulate these attributes of God? How might this reveal "making God in the image of man"? Who does this reveal that you are emulating (out of admiration or fear) other than God?

6. How does your understanding of, rest in, and emulation of this quadrant of attributes compare to that of the other three quadrants? How balanced is your view of God (a circle, an oval, or a blob)?

7. What changes do you need to make to understand or rely upon these attributes of God more? What specific actions (i.e., repentance, study, changing life patterns, or learning new skills) will this require? Who is holding you accountable? Whose advice or counsel are you seeking?

8. How would you summarize the changes in your view of God as a result of this week's study? What hope, relief, joy, or fear of the Lord has emerged from those changes?

The Main Point

Take time to praise God for how effortlessly he manifests all these qualities. Our struggles to rest in and emulate God's character should serve to increase our level of awe and deep appreciation for the God we have the privilege of serving. As you study Scripture, sing hymns and songs, interact with people, and live in creation, look and listen for these attributes. Praise God when you find them.

CONCLUSION

In a day of information overload and societal ADD, going back through a study like this—after first reading it as an article—to carefully examine yourself and reflect on God's character is highly countercultural. But it is worth it.

As you prepare to devote an extended period of time to examining God's attributes and your life in light of them, consider the following quote from Maurice Roberts for encouragement:

> Our age has been sadly deficient in what may be termed spiritual greatness. At the root of this is the modern disease of shallowness. We are all too impatient to meditate on the faith we profess. . . . Rather, it is unhurried meditation on gospel truths and the exposing of our minds to these truths that yields the fruit of sanctified character.[1]

---

1. Maurice Roberts, "O the Depth!", *Banner of Truth*, July 1990, 2.